The Christmas Ass

by Jana Enloe
illustrated by Z. Pullen

Between 2 Commas, LLC
Houston • Tokyo

The holidays were drawing near
and hearts were open wide
as the Bunny family talked
about the joy of Christmastime.

In the kitchen, Grandma
cooked family favorites and baked.
She added sprinkles to cookies
and frosted fancy carrot cake.

Mother and Father cleaned the den and decorated with glee. They hung tinsel and glittering lights on the tall Christmas tree.

With the sun shining down
and snow on the ground,
and the children yearning for Christmas Day,
they could hardly contain their excitement,
so they were sent outside to play.

Little brother Rex built a snow bunny,
and JJ sang a song and swayed.
Risa skated on the river,
while Bae giggled and threw snowballs
as she hid behind the sleigh.

The oldest, JJ, had made it clear
that she wanted specific gifts for Christmas this year.
A sparkling purple purse was at the top of her list.
A porcelain baby doll and jewelry were also her wish.

Father found a baby doll that he thought was just right. He wrapped it up for JJ and placed it out of sight.

Mother found a necklace with little black stones. She knew that JJ would love to have some jewelry of her own.

Risa and Rex searched far and wide. They found a plain purple purse for JJ that their piggybanks could provide.

It was finally Christmas Eve,
and the family was fast asleep.
All except for JJ,
who didn't sleep a wink.

With the stars above twinkling,
and the moon bright and low,
JJ dreamed of presents
wrapped in shiny silver bows.

Christmas morning was finally here!
The family opened gifts
with excitement and cheer.

"Oh thank you!" said Risa.
"Just what I wanted!" shouted Rex.
Bae squealed with delight,
"My gift is the best!"

JJ's first gift to open
was the black necklace from Mother.
JJ said, "I only wear gold.
Couldn't you have gotten me another?"

Father's present was next,
the sweet baby doll.

"This is not the kind I wanted at all."

Father was fed up.
"That's it!" he said to JJ.
"Into my room. Now!
I have something important to say."

Father said, "Everyone attempted
to give you a gift to please,
but you forgot the most important part—
how to receive."

His eyes softened as he said,
"I'm sorry to be crass,
but you have become The Christmas Ass.

"You see, for many years
I was called The Christmas Ass too,
and this donkey was given to me,
that I'm now giving to you.

"It's a reminder," Father said,
"to think before speaking next year,"
and he pulled JJ close,
as her eyes filled with tears.

Hand in hand,
they walked back down the hall.
JJ sniffed and told her family,
"I was selfish.
I am sorry to all."

Then the whole family
gathered for a big bunny hug,
and JJ was assured
that she would always be loved.

Their ears closely listened,
and this is what they heard
as Father explained
with a prayer and a word,
"JJ has learned an important lesson today
about how to receive gifts
in a more gracious way,
and there's nothing any of you could do or say
to take our love for you away.

"Now out to the village we will go
to spread this message to others we know."

With gifts perched atop,
the family crowded onto the sleigh,
and Father called out joyfully,
"Blessings to all this Christmas Day!"

A Note from Grandma

*We have all heard the Christmas saying,
"It is better to give than to receive,"
but The Christmas Ass didn't think like that.
It was always "me, me, me!"*

*When given a gift that didn't make her shout,
she would sit in the corner and do nothing but pout.*

*As Christmastime neared, the family would fear
that this selfish behavior would reappear.*

*When she realized what she had done,
she apologized for ruining everyone's fun.*

*So all was restored by a love with no end
and a lesson learned that she'd like to extend:*

*"Hold onto your donkey, put selfish thoughts away,
and learn to receive gifts in a gracious way.*

*"And whatever you do, don't let this Christmas pass,
with you being named The Christmas Ass."*

For my husband and our precious children.
May you always remember I love you, no matter what.
—J. E.

For Renate and Hudson, the two greatest gifts. Much love.
—Z. P.

Text copyright © 2020 Jana Enloe
Illustrations copyright © 2020 Zachary Pullen
Design by Lois Rainwater
All rights reserved
This book was proudly produced by Book Bridge Press
www.bookbridgepress.com

No part of this book may be reproduced in any manner without express written consent of the publisher, except in the case of brief excerpts in critical reviews and articles. All inquiries or sales requests should be addressed to:

Between 2 Commas, LLC
TheChristmasAss@gmail.com
www.TheChristmasAss.com

Printed and bound in the United States of America
First Edition
10 9 8 7 6 5 4 3 2 1
LCCN 2020908572
ISBN 978-0-578-69263-0